# INTJ PERSONALITY - HARNESS YOUR GIFTS, UTILIZE YOUR STRENGTHS, FIND SUCCESS, AND THRIVE AS THE UNSTOPPABLE MASTERMIND

*THE ULTIMATE GUIDE TO THE INTJ PERSONALITY TYPE INCLUDING: INTJ CAREERS, INTJ PERSONALITY TRAITS, INTJ RELATIONSHIPS, AND FAMOUS INTJS*

*FIND HEALTH, WEALTH, AND HAPPINESS AS AN INTJ*

*DAN JOHNSTON*

Published by Dan Johnston

www.DreamsAroundTheWorld.com

# CONTENTS

# WHY YOU SHOULD READ THIS BOOK

You know those people for whom everything just seems so easy?

Their career or business is always getting better. Their relationships appear happy and fulfilling. They have a satisfying home life, work life, and, by damn, never seem to have a complaint in the world. **Let's call these people the "Thrivers."**

Then there are those for whom life feels like a constant upward swim. At work, they feel like they don't belong. Their relationships are either problematic or unsatisfying. To them, life has always been a struggle. Let's call them the Strugglers.

What's going on here? Are some of us just blessed with good fortune? Is everyone else just cursed with constant struggle?

Don't worry, there are no magical forces at work – just some psychology. It's been my experience that there is only one difference between the Strugglers and the Thrivers.

The Thrivers, by reflection, study, or just dumb luck, have built their lives around their natural personalities. Their work utilizes their strengths while their relationships complement their weaknesses.

A small percentage of the Thrivers came into their lives "naturally." The careers their parents or teachers recommended were the perfect fit for them or they had a gut feeling that turned out to be right. They met their ideal partner who complemented them perfectly. I believe, however, that this group is the minority.

Most Thrivers have spent years "watching" themselves and reflecting about who they really are. For some, this is a natural process. For others (myself included), it's a more deliberate process. We read, studied, questioned, and took tests all in the name of self-awareness. We've made it a priority to know and understand ourselves.

Whatever a Thriver learns about themselves, they use to make significant changes in their lives. They change careers, end relationships, and start new hobbies. They do all this so that one day their lives will be fulfilled and will have a natural flow: a life in which they can thrive.

This book is for Thrivers: past, present, and future.

If you once had your flow but can't seem to find it again, read on.

If you're in your flow and want to keep and improve it, read on.

And if you're one of the beautiful souls struggling but committed to finding your flow and to thrive, you're in the right place. Read on.

Today you may feel like a salmon swimming upstream, but this is a temporary state. One day soon, you will find yourself evolving. Perhaps into a dolphin, swimming among those with whom you belong, free to be yourself, to play, and to enjoy life. Maybe you'd rather find your place as a whale - wise and powerful, roaming the oceans and setting your own path, respected and admired by all.

## KNOWLEDGE BRINGS AWARENESS AND AWARENESS BRINGS SUCCESS

I'm an entrepreneur as well as a writer. As an entrepreneur, negotiation plays a big part in any success I might have. One of the secrets to being a good negotiator is always to be the one in the room with the most information.

The same holds true for decision making in our personal lives. When it comes to the big things in life, we can't make a good decision if we don't have all the relevant information.

I think most of us understand this on an external level. When we're shopping for a new car, we research our options: the prices, the engines, and the warranties. We find out as much as we can to help make our decision.

Unfortunately, we often forget the most important factor in our decisions: Us.

A Ford Focus is a better economic decision and a more enjoyable drive than an SUV...but that doesn't matter if you're seven feet tall or have five kids who need to be driven to hockey in the snow.

When it comes to life decisions, such as our work or relationships, who we are is the most important decision factor.

It doesn't matter if all your friends say he is the perfect guy; it only matters if he's perfect for you. It doesn't matter if your family wants you to be a lawyer, a doctor, or an accountant.... What do you want to do? If you make your decision based on what the outside world says, you won't find the levels of happiness or fulfillment you desire.

IF YOU MAKE YOUR DECISION BASED ON WHAT THE OUTSIDE WORLD SAYS, YOU WON'T FIND THE LEVELS OF HAPPINESS OR FULFILLMENT YOU DESIRE.

In order to make the best decisions for you, you must first know yourself. That is the purpose of this book: to provide the most in-depth information on your personality type, the INFP, available anywhere.

## By reading this book you will:

- Improve self-awareness.
- Uncover your natural strengths.
- Understand your weaknesses.
- Discover new career opportunities.
- Learn how to have better relationships.
- Develop a greater understanding of your family, partner, and friends.
- Have the knowledge to build your ideal life around your natural personality.
- Have more happiness, health, love, money, and all around life success while feeling more focused and fulfilled.

# FREE READER-ONLY EXCLUSIVES: WORKBOOK AND BONUSES

When I wrote this book, I set out to create the most *useful* guide available. I know there will always be bigger or more detailed textbooks out there, but how many of them are actually helpful?

To help you get the most from this book, I have created a collection of free extras to support you along the way. To download these, simply visit the special section of my website: www.PersonalityTypesTraining.com/thrive

You will be asked to enter your email address so I can send you the "Thriving Bonus Pack." You'll receive:

1. A 5-part mini-course (delivered via email) with tips on how to optimize your life so you can maximize your strengths and thrive.
2. A compatibility chart showing how you are most likely to relate to the other 15 personality types. You'll discover which people are likely to become good friends (or better) and whom you should avoid at all cost.
3. A PDF workbook to ramp up the results you'll get from this book. It's formatted to be printed, so you can fill in your answers to the exercises in each chapter as you go.

To download the Thriving Bonus Pack, visit:

www.PersonalityTypesTraining.com/thrive

# DISCLAIMER

I know this book will serve you well in discovering your strengths and building your self-awareness. I have researched and written this book based on years of practical experience including running multiple businesses, talking to dozens of people about their strengths and weaknesses, and applying this knowledge to my own life to discover my strengths and build a business around what I do best. With that said, I must emphasize that I am not a psychologist, psychiatrist, or counselor, or in any way qualified to offer medical advice. The information in this book is intended to improve your life but it does not replace professional advice in any way, nor is it legal, medical, or psychiatric advice. So, if you're in a bad place or may be suffering from a mental illness, please seek professional help!

# INTRODUCTION TO THIS SERIES

The goal of this series is to provide a clear window into the strengths, weaknesses, opportunities, and challenges of each type.

You'll discover new things about yourself and find new ways to tap into your strengths and create a life where you thrive. I want you to have every advantage possible in the areas of work, play, relationships, health, and finance.

This book is part of a series; each one focuses on one "type." You will find that I write directly to you, although I do not make an assumption as to your personality type or your traits. I will generally refer to the type, aka INTJ, instead of saying "you." Not every trait of a specific type applies to everyone of that type, and we never want to make any assumptions about who you are or about your limitations.

I would recommend beginning with your type to learn most about yourself, but don't stop there. Each book focuses on a particular type and will be valuable for that type, but will be equally valuable for family, friends, bosses, and colleagues of that type.

Even before writing these books, I found myself doing extensive reading on the types of my brother, parents, friends, and even dates. In my business, I would research the types of my assistants, employees, and potential business partners. I found that learning about myself got me 60% of the way, and the other 40% came from learning about the other people in my life.

If you plan to read up on all the different types, I suggest looking at my "Collection" books, which include multiple types all in one book for a reduced price. It'll be easier and a better price for you than buying each individual book.

You'll find a link to all the other books in this series at the end of this book.

# ADVICE FROM INTJS FOR INTJS

After publishing the first edition of this book, I reached out to a group of INTJs. I asked them what advice they would share with a younger, perhaps less experienced INTJ, that would help them live the best life possible.

I thought I would include them in this updated edition, and what better way to kick things off?

You can learn a lot about a type by what they say, and also by how they say it. So, allow me to present a few of their inspiring and mostly unedited answers here. You'll find the rest towards the end of the book.

*"I know the things in your head are much more interesting than what happens outside, but try to get out of your little world more."*

*"1. Introversion is not a pathological condition. Enjoy finding peaceful spaces.*

*2. Learn where your intuition comes from. Once you know that, you may learn to trust and use it.*

*3. Wait until you hit 20 before planning global domination and building your own hollowed-out volcanic lair.*

*4. There is much wisdom in 'Pinky and the Brain'...."*

*"Always be yourself and objective."*

*"Feelings are not illogical. Just because your brain says you "can" do something, doesn't mean you really want to. Realizing what you feel enjoyment in doing is just as important as logically following a less enjoyable path." (45-year-old INTJ)*

*"Master 'efficiency' in your learning abilities, and find your core 'motivation.' These two features will help you out immensely in the real world to succeed in EVERYTHING that you wish to obtain."*

*"When looking for someone of the opposite sex, you should find someone you aren't just drawn to physically and emotionally, but someone you could spend a week with in a fallout shelter just talking to and not getting bored."*

*"There aren't a lot of people like you, but they wish there were, even though they can't figure you out!? Make smiling a habit. Invest in Apple & Microsoft. Oh, and most importantly, study Nikola Tesla. He's the only one that understood and will explain it all." (43-year-old INTJ)*

*"The wiser you get, the more you realize you wish you could ask your younger self for advice."*

*"Above all things, being comfortable in your own skin will help you to be successful."*

*"Learn social skills as soon as possible. Avoid getting immersed in the nihilist INTJ mentality. Try and be happier and comfortable with feelings."*

*"Travel, travel, travel!"*

*"Life is experiential, and if you're anything like me, you'll learn more from your own stumbles and successes than you'll find in writing here. My opinion? Nine tenths of what makes life worth living is figuring things out as we go. Have fun with it."*

*"Your intuition is going to be right about 95% of the time, so don't ignore/dismiss it, no matter how badly you want something to work out."*

# INTRODUCTION TO MYERS-BRIGGS®

I first officially discovered personality psychology about five years ago. I say officially because I do have some vague memories of taking a career test in high school that was likely based on the Myers-Briggs® instrument, but who really pays attention to tests when you are 16?

The Myers-Briggs assessment is one of many options in the world of personality profiles and testing. It is arguably the most popular, and in my opinion it is the best place to start. I say this because the results provide insight into all aspects of our lives, whereas other tests are often focused on just career.

The Myers-Briggs instrument is based on the idea that people are quite different from one another. These differences go deeper than emotions, moods, or environment, and speak to how we're actually wired to behave.

And, as it turns out, most people end up being wired 1 of 16 ways, based on four groups of characteristics.

This doesn't mean we can't build certain traits or change our behavior. Rather, knowing your personality type is an opportunity to learn which traits come most naturally to you and which areas you may find challenging or need to invest time in developing.

Your type provides a platform to understand yourself and create a plan for personal growth based on your unique personality strengths and weaknesses.

It is also an opportunity to understand the people around you and get to the root of many conflicts. In fact, you may find that understanding the different types and how others relate to you is the most valuable aspect of the Myers-Briggs instrument.

# THE 16 TYPES AND 4 GROUPS

In total there are 16 different personality types that are described by a unique series of 4 letters.

At first, the types appear confusing, but they're really quite simple.

Each type is based on one of two modes of being or thinking for each of the four letters.

E (extrovert) or I (introvert)

N (intuitive) or S (sensing)

T (thinking) or F (feeling)

P (perceiving) or J (judging)

Now, don't pay too much attention to the words tied to each letter because they don't actually offer a great description for the characteristic.

In just a second, I'll share my explanation for each letter. But just before this, I want to share an important point to remember: Personality analysis and profiling is a bit of an art, as well as a science. In other words, since people are so diverse, the descriptions and results aren't always black and white. Some people have a strong preference for one mode or the other, but others are closer to the middle. It's natural for all of us occasionally to feel or demonstrate traits of the other types.

What we want to focus on here is your natural way of being and the functions you are strongest in. It is also important to know that you can, and will, develop your secondary (or auxiliary) and third (or tertiary) "functions" over time and with practice. In doing so, you will create a more balanced personality with fewer weak spots and a more diverse set of skills. In fact, the key to overcoming most personality challenges is to develop your weaker functions.

Generally, it's said that we grow our primary function in our early years, our secondary function in our twenties and thirties, and our third function some time in our thirties and forties. However, this assumes you're not being proactive nor are reading a book like this one. In your case, there is no reason you can't leap ahead a few decades and strengthen your other functions ahead of schedule.

## WHAT THE FOUR LETTERS MEAN

As you know, there are four letters that make up your personality type.

At first, these letters can be a little confusing, especially since their descriptions aren't the most telling.

Here's how I explain each letter.

### For the first letter in your type, you are either an E or an I.

The E or I describes how we relate with other people and social situations.

Extroverts are drawn to people, groups, and new social situations. They are generally comfortable at parties and in large groups.

Introverts are more reserved. This is not to say that introverts do not enjoy people, they do. Introverts are just happier in smaller groups, and with people they know and trust, like friends or family. Keep in mind, this does not mean that introverts are not capable of mastering social skills if they must. Rather, they will not be drawn to such situations or find the process as exciting or enjoyable as an extrovert would.

"The Deal Breaker": For some people E or I is obvious. For

others, the line is blurred. This question will make your preference clear: "Does being around new people or groups add to or drain your energy? If you spent an entire day alone would you feel "off" or bad, or would you be just fine?" If you can spend a day or two alone without feeling bad, or if spending a few hours in a group of people leaves you feeling tired, well then, you're an introvert.

While extroverts may often steal a lot of the attention in a room, introverts often have the upper hand. While many extroverts crave the spotlight, introverts are able to sit back and calmly observe, learning more about a situation and making their contributions more meaningful and impactful.

Further, introverts have the ability to work alone for long periods. In many professions, such as writing, this is a significant advantage.

INTJs are introverts. This is why INTJs are so capable at working alone, are self-sufficient, and usually not interested in building large social groups.

## For the second letter, you are either an N or an S.

This trait describes how you interact with the world.

Those with the intuitive trait (N) tend to be introspective and imaginative. They enjoy theoretical discussions and "big picture" kind of ideas. For an extreme example, imagine a philosophy professor with a stained suit jacket and a terribly messy office.

Of course, this isn't the reality for most N's. Most intuitive people live a happy, fulfilled life full of new ideas and inspirations...all while managing the day-to-day aspects of their lives at an acceptable level. N's have an exceptional imagination and ability to form new ideas, tell stories, and inspire those around them.

Those with the sensor trait are observant and in touch with their immediate environment. They prefer practical, "hands on" information to theory. They prefer facts over ideas. For an extreme example, think of a mechanic or military strategist.

INTJs have the intuitive trait. This is why they are drawn to ideas and have a great imagination and ability to problem solve.

## Third, you are either a T or an F.

This trait describes how you make decisions and come to conclusions, as well as what role emotions play in your personality and how you deal with them.

Those with the thinker trait are "tough-minded." They tend to be objective and impersonal with others. This can make them appear uncaring, but they are generally very fair. Those with the thinking trait rely on logic and rational arguments for their decisions. The "T" trait would be common among (successful) investors and those who need to make impersonal and objective decisions in their careers.

Those with the feeler trait are personal, friendly, and sympathetic to others. Their decisions are often influenced by their emotions or the "people" part of a situation. They are also more sensitive and affected by their emotions, and less afraid to show their emotions to the outside world. The "F" trait would be common among counselors and psychologists.

INTJs have the thinker trait. This is why INTJs can be so logical. It is also why INTJs may have trouble empathizing or connecting with more emotional people.

## Lastly, you are either a P or a J.

This trait describes how you organize information in your internal and external worlds. This translates into how you schedule yourself, stay organized, and evaluate your options.

Perceivers are best described as "Probers" or "Explorers." They look for options, opportunities, and alternatives. This means they tend to be more creative, open-minded, and, well, often have messy bedrooms. They're happy to give one plan a try without having all the details beforehand, knowing they can adjust or try something else in the future.

Judgers are structured and organized. They tend to be more consistent and scheduled. Spreadsheets may be their friends and their rooms will be clean...or at least organized. They prefer concrete plans and closure over openness and possibilities.

You would find more P's among artists and creative groups, whereas professions like accountants and engineers would be dominated by J's.

INTJs have the judging trait. This is one reason they are able to stay organized, focused, and disciplined while working towards a goal. Of those with the judging trait, INTJs are a bit of an exception and are often very creative and open to new ideas...as long as the data is there to support it.

## THE FOUR GROUPS

Since the original creation of the 16 types, psychologists have recognized four distinct groups, each containing four types. The four types within each group have distinct traits in common based on sharing two of the four traits.

- The four types are:
- The Artisans (The SPs)
- The Guardians (The SJs)
- The Idealists (The NFs)
- The Rationals (The NTs)

**As an INTJ, you are a Rational.**

A Rational's greatest strength is strategy. They are intellectual in speech, and utilitarian in how they pursue their goals.

They are seekers of knowledge and trust reason and logic over emotion and feelings. They seek to gain as much information as possible and apply this knowledge towards long-term plans for achieving their goals.

Not known for their empathy, Rationals are considered tough-minded in how they deal with others. The truth is, Rationals strive to be honest and fair in their decision-making and in how they treat people. So, even though they may come off as cold or uncaring, their actual decisions are usually very fair and objective.

The other three Rational types, your cousins, are:

- The Fieldmarshals and Executives: ENTJs
- The Charming Visionary: ENTPs
- The Thinker and Architect: INTPs


To learn more about how all the types relate and interact, download the free compatibility chart at:

www.PersonalityTypesTraining.com/thrive

# INTJ'S FOUR FUNCTIONS

It is important for you to know what the INTJ's four functions are, even if you don't yet know the science behind them. According to the Myers-Briggs instrument, all types have the same four functions: intuition, sensing, thinking, and feeling. The differences are in how the individual uses the function (introverted vs extroverted), and the order in which the functions serve as strengths.

This will all make more sense as you read this book and continue your studies.

If it helps to get you started, here is my best attempt to explain the four functions in human terms. Many online resources use confusing technical language and psych speak when explaining this. I'll try to do the opposite here.

Think of the four functions as your four potential superpowers. Like an RPG videogame, your starting character has certain potential abilities you can gain access to as you grow. If you select the Elf, you will have access to different powers than the Orc or the Knight.

## The eight available functions are:

- Extroverted Intuition (Ne)
- Introverted Intuition (Ni)
- Extroverted Sensing (Se)
- Introverted Sensing (Si)
- Extroverted Feeling (Fe)
- Introverted Feeling (Fi)
- Extroverted Thinking (Te)
- Introverted Thinking (Ti)

Note that the E or I attached to each function is not an

indicator of the individual's preference to introversion or extroversion. Rather, it is an indicator of how they use the particular function.

Which four functions a type has, and the order in which they are strengths, is determined by the types preferences on the Extroversion vs Introversion, and Perceiving vs Judging measures. I'm going to leave it there, as any explanation beyond this would give us both a psychology jargon headache.

In your early years, your personality is ruled by your dominant function. This shapes your early strengths as well as weaknesses. Over time, through challenge and experience, you develop your second (auxiliary) and third (tertiary) "functions." You create a more powerful and balanced personality. You minimize weak spots, mature emotionally, and develop a diverse set of skills.

**The key to overcoming most personality challenges is developing (strengthening) the weaker functions.**

In general, we grow our primary (or dominant) function in our early years, our secondary function in our twenties and thirties, and our third function some time in our thirties and forties. However, this assumes you're not being proactive or reading a book like this one. In your case, there is no reason you can't leap ahead a few decades and strengthen your other functions ahead of schedule. Actually, doing so is essential to your personal development.

## How We Use Our Functions

In the following section, you will notice each function is described as either introverted or extroverted. This is an indicator of use.

For example, an INFJ has "introverted intuition." This means they use their intuition to internally process ideas and situations and come to conclusions. Their secondary function is "extroverted feeling." This means they interact with the outside world using their feeling function. It also means most inputs are filed through the INFJ's feeling function before reaching their intuition.

ENFPs have "extroverted intuition" as their dominant function. This means the ENFP interacts with and experiences the outside world using their intuition. For an ENFP, their secondary function is "introverted feeling." This means the ENFP processes their thoughts and judgments internally based on their feelings.

An INTJ has the following functions:

**Dominant Function - Introverted Intuition (Ni):** INTJs use their intuition to internally process situations and ideas. This is their most natural function and gives them many of their visionary and creative abilities.

**Auxiliary Function - Extroverted Thinking (Te):** This is an INTJ's second strongest function and one they must actively develop in their 20s and 30s in order to create a well-rounded personality. Te strives to be efficient and productive through organization and scheduling. Te is all about logic, seeking the root cause for an action, as well as spotting faulty reasoning.

**Tertiary Function - Introverted Feeling (Fi):** This is the INTJ's third function and is used to interpret and judge the outside world against an internal set of values built around harmony and authenticity. Developing this function will give an INTJ the ability to read between the lines and sense what is false or inauthentic in a situation.

**Inferior Function - Extroverted Sensing (Se):** The Se function happens in the sensations and experience of the immediate, physical world. INTJs that develop this function may see benefits in all areas of life because of the mind-body connection. Some ways to develop this function include sports, spending time in nature, and building real physical objects, such as models or furniture.

# DISCOVERING THE MASTERMIND: WHO IS AN INTJ?

At this point, I'm going to assume you're an INTJ and are reading about yourself, or reading about someone you care about who is an INTJ.

I'm also going to assume you've read some of the basic descriptions online about INTJs and have bought this book because you want depth and details on how INTJs can thrive.

So with that, I won't bore you with a drawn out description of INTJs. I'll keep it short and let you get on to the other chapters where we go deeper into specific areas like career and relationships.

INTJs are reserved, reflective, and rational. They are also bright and intelligent, clear-headed, and pragmatic in their approach to life.

At the core of the INTJ personality is independence and a desire for efficiency. An INTJ is at their best and most creative when they have autonomy.

INTJs have a deep desire for expression, particularly the expression of their own intellectual designs. They have a gift for analyzing and articulating complex ideas and theories.

INTJs excel at brainstorming new approaches to situations and problem solving. In fact, they are the best of all types at this.

INTJs can be great leaders, but they will not push for the role. Rather, an INTJ will step into a leadership role when they feel they are the best person suited for the position, and perhaps the only person capable of succeeding.

In their decision making, INTJs are decisive while still open to new ideas if the facts or situations change. Ultimately, they strive to make the best and most efficient decision for the situation, regardless of their personal opinions or interests.

INTJs love to solve complex problems. They tend to make positive statements over negative ones and focus on future improvements instead of past mistakes.

INTJs do well in occupations within academia, research, science, engineering, consulting, management, and law.

# IN GOOD COMPANY:
# FAMOUS INFPS

As an INTJ, you are among some very good company. In this chapter you'll find a collection of famous and "successful" people who are either confirmed, or suspected, as being INTJs.

Do not use this chapter as a guide to what you must do or whom you must resemble. Rather, use this chapter as a source of inspiration. It is a chance to see what's possible as an INTJ and what great things have been accomplished by those who share a similar makeup to you.

Personally, I have found great value in studying famous people from my own type, including reading their autobiographies. Most of us spend the early years of our lives feeling lost and trying to figure out our purpose or how we want to end up. I've found studying those of my type who have found their purpose, and then success, gives me a shortcut to understanding my own potential and the directions my life could go.

## FAMOUS INTJS

### Scientists, Writers, and Thought Leaders

- Isaac Newton
- Karl Marx
- John Nash (mathematician)
- H.L. Mencken (journalist)
- Ayn Rand
- Isaac Asimov
- Christopher Hitchens (journalist)
- Friedrich Nietzsche

- John Maynard Keynes
- Heraclitus (Greek philosopher)
- Nikola Tesla
- Jane Austen
- Stephen Hawking
- Ted Kaczynski
- Jay-Z

## Actors and Performers

- Bobby Fischer (chess champion)
- Garry Kasparov (chess champion)
- Arnold Schwarzenegger
- James Cameron
- Russell Crowe
- Jay-Z
- Julia Stiles
- Jodie Foster

## Politicians

- Mark Zuckerberg
- John Adams
- Vladimir Lenin
- Arnold Schwarzenegger
- Jay-Z
- Augustus

Yes, I put Jay-Z in all three categories. Read up on the man and tell me he isn't a writer, thought leader and philosopher, a performer, and a business leader, all wrapped up in one.

*Worth Noting:* If you haven't yet read up on any of the other types, you may not notice the distinctions of the famous INTJs. Compared with other types, you may notice that famous INTJs tend to become the best at what they do, pushing the limits of what is possible. They're able to blend creative talents with business abilities and a strong drive to "produce" more of whatever they do. They are also very strategic in their thinking and how they plan their lives. For an excellent example of this, read Arnold Schwarzenegger's autobiography, "Total Recall: My Unbelievably True Life Story." I've read and listened to this book. Not only is it really entertaining, it also contains a ton of insights on INTJs.

## GOING DEEPER EXERCISE

Of the famous INTJs on this list, which are most familiar to you?

_____

_____

_____

_____

What are some common elements you notice? These could be specific personality traits or characteristics. It could also include actions they have taken or tough decisions they have made. For example: going against the grain or choosing to follow a passion.

_____

_____

_____

_____

_____

# YOUR SECRET WEAPONS

## (Aka your unique strengths)

In my own life, I have found no greater success secret than discovering, *and applying*, my strengths.

When we are young, we're often taught that we need to be good at many things. For example, success in school is based on your average grade. Most parents would much prefer their child have a smooth report card of all B+s than two A+s and two C-s.

The real world doesn't reward the well-rounded individual, at least not exceptionally well. Those who receive the greatest rewards are those who focus on their strengths and ignore all else. Think of people like Arnold Schwarzenegger, Steve Jobs, and Oprah Winfrey.

Does anyone *really* care if Oprah is bad at math, if Arnold has trouble managing his personal life, or if Steve Jobs was a bit of an ass to employees from time to time?

Nope. No one cares because each of these Greats focused on their strengths and created an extraordinary life for themselves.

Oprah (an ENFJ) harnessed her empathy and ability to build trust and bond with people to create incredible interviews and connect with her audience.

Arnold (an INTJ) used his focus, discipline, and strategic thinking to achieve incredible goals in fitness, performing, and politics, despite being the underdog in almost everything he ever did.

Steve Jobs (an ISTP) kept his energy focused on his creative and visual strengths. His vision was so clear, and his innovations so impressive, that his social graces didn't matter.

Now, as you read on, you will discover the unique strengths

closely linked to INTJs. While you read this, remember that these are the strengths that come naturally to you, but you still need to develop and fine-tune them if you want to thrive.

INTJs' strengths revolve around their people skills. INTJs are exceptional at understanding and connecting with others in a positive way.

## AN INTJ'S SECRET WEAPONS

- Thinking big and creating new ideas.
- INTJs can understand complex theories AND convert them into practical strategic plans.
- Overall, INTJs are very intelligent.
- INTJs are OK with conflict and have no problem addressing issues head on.
- They're usually confident, independent, and self-assured.
- The INTJ's mind is naturally set up to systematically analyze information from multiple sources and perspectives. They are able to sort and filter this information, and then apply it to solving real world problems or developing new strategies. This is an exceptionally powerful gift.
- They're able to see connections and patterns that most others miss. This often leads them to create new ideas.
- INTJs are not attached to their ideas or opinions. If a better approach comes up, they have no problem changing direction and adopting a new idea. In other words, they don't let their personal ego get in the way of the greater good or what is "right."
- INTJs are intelligent and have no problem focusing. This gives them an ability to grasp difficult ideas and work on one thing until completion.
- INTJs commit to finishing what they start. If they take on a project or goal they will focus and work on it until they

reach their desired outcome. INTJs aren't afraid of hard work and their persistence is genuinely inspiring to others.

• Thinking of new ways to do things others have missed.

## Highly developed INTJs will enjoy even more superpowers:

• An ability to understand a complex and difficult goal and create an ingenious system and plan of action for attaining it. This ability makes them outstanding strategists (business or military), scientists, and doctors.

• Being genius (literally) problem solvers. INTJs who combine their logical abilities, persistence, and ability to deeply understand a topic have an incredible gift.

INTJs are the most likely of all types to create new solutions to problems that plague society, such as diseases or environmental issues.

Many breakthroughs in the science and technical worlds have come from the minds of INTJs.

• An impressive ability to understand very difficult concepts beyond what their "natural intelligence" would otherwise be able to understand.

• Once an INTJ has attained a certain level of life experience and wisdom, they may become powerful forces in business and the political arena. Need I reference Arnold Schwarzenegger again?

## In summary, a developed INFP can be:

- Goal Oriented
- Very Driven and Determined
- Persistent
- Insightful
- Creative
- Intelligent
- Logical
- Focused
- Quick
- Caring
- Intuitive
- Supportive
- Inspiring
- Ingenious
- Innovative

## Keys To Using Your Strengths as an INFP

1. Make time to spend with people and allow your mind to relax. Often it is during this "down time" when the best ideas are formulated.

2. Focus on goals that will bring a balanced happiness to your life.

3. Realize you're unique among most groups and learn to accept others (and their weaknesses).

4. It's easy to get trapped in your head or your ideas. Start a hobby or activity that involves something physical, such as a sport, outdoor activity, or artistic craft. This will help you get out of your head and connect your ideas with the world around you.

In this and future chapters, you will discover "Going Deeper" exercises. These are designed to help you better understand and apply the chapter's content. If you're like me, you may want to write down your answers. When you bought this book you also got access to a companion workbook you can print and then fill in with your answers as you go. You can download the workbook for free at:

www.PersonalityTypesTraining.com/thrive

## GOING DEEPER EXERCISE

Of the strengths listed above, which most jump out at you as strengths of your own?

_____

_____

_____

_____

_____

What are three strengths listed above that you know you have but are not actively using in your life, at least not as much as you know you should?

_____

_____

_____

_____

_____

How could you apply these strengths more frequently?

_____

_____

_____

_____

_____

# YOUR KRYPTONITE

## (Aka your potential weaknesses)

You didn't think I was going to stop at your strengths, did you? As much as I say *focus on your strengths*, it is still important to be aware of your weaknesses, even if it is just so you can ignore them more easily.

Below, you will find a collection of weaknesses, or challenges, common among INTJs. As with strengths, this is not a definitive list and do not take it as a prescription for how INTJs have to be.

Sometimes I will see posts in a Facebook group for a specific type where people seem overly proud of their type challenges. I remember one post on an ENFP group making light of how the poster had been unable to tidy their room in four days. While it was good for a "we've all been there" chuckle, I did find myself turned off when I thought about what a chaotic life this person must have.

This person chose not to fix their weakness. For example, they could have chosen to develop their self-discipline and, over time, it would become easier to stay tidy. They were also unwilling to just accept this weakness and find another solution. If they decided to embrace it, then they could have just hired a maid. Instead, they chose to suffer what they described as four days of agony simply trying to clean a room.

Many of the INTJs' challenges tend to revolve around their dominant function (introverted intuition) being overdeveloped to the point where it takes over. Then  the other functions, such as how they interact with the world (extroverted thinking), are used to serve their internal thoughts and judgments. This means perceiving everything with confirmation bias, trying to justify or "back up" what they already know instead of objectively looking for new information.

As you read these, remember they are only a result of an underdeveloped personality and can easily be overcome by developing weaker areas.

If some of these weaknesses don't really resonate with you, that's **good**. Do not assume you should be weak in an area simply because you read it here. It is very possible that you are wired a little differently, or that you've already developed beyond some of your inborn weak spots.

On the other hand, if you find yourself nodding in agreement while reading, take it as an opportunity to either improve that area of yourself, or accept it and find another way to deal with it.

*Note: You'll find more on "outsourcing" your weaknesses in the later chapter "Practical Problems to Common Challenges."*

## COMMON KRYPTONITE FOR THE INTJ

Before they fully develop their personalities, some INTJs may:

- Unleash extreme emotions when under stress, far more than the situation calls for.
- Be very impatient with less intelligent people, or those who disagree with their way of doing things.
- Become pigheaded and ignore other people's opinions. This comes from both their mode of operating and interacting with the world, as well as experience. INTJs are very intelligent and are perfectionists. So, more often than not, they are right.
- Turn finding fault in others into a "game" and take pleasure in criticizing others. This is a recipe for personal unhappiness.
- Have little regard for how others see them or how they

are valued. This can lead to harsh treatment and offensive behaviors or comments.

- INTJs are perfectionists with very high standards and expectations. This can lead to unrealistic (and unfair) expectations of themselves as well as of others. Their high expectations of themselves have a positive side effect – their drive. But this can also lead to them to being far too hard on themselves. Their high expectations of others can have a motivating effect, but can also lead to excessive pressure.
- INTJs can be "harsh" in their judgments and treatment of other people. This can play out in many different ways:
  o This is especially true if they feel they've been wronged. In this case, they can often hold grudges far too long and have a lot of trouble forgiving people.
  o They may forget their sense of empathy and become intolerant and overly judgmental of weaknesses in other people. INTJs should remember that these people would part ways with their weaknesses if they could.
  o They can get angry or impatient with people who don't "get it" or appear to be doing things wrong.
  o They can be very pointed and cruel with their words without regard for the hurt they could cause.
- Have trouble expressing their inner thoughts and feelings with other people.
- Have trouble and not know how to act in situations that require decisiveness.

## OVERCOMING YOUR WEAKNESSES

Many of the INTJs' weaknesses share a single root cause. If they do not develop their secondary function, extroverted thinking, INTJs' other functions can become slave to their introverted intuition. This can skew or distort everything they experience in order to serve the beliefs of their introverted thinking (and prove they are "right").

If they do not develop their secondary function, "extroverted thinking," the INTJs tend to "know what is right" before really thinking about the issue.

OK, sorry, that was a lot of "psych speak." Let me translate. INTJs tend to judge things too fast based on what they intuitively think is right. To overcome their weaknesses, INTJs first need to take a little more time to think about people, situations, or ideas, and then see if there is new information that would change what they think is "right."

Think and process first, judge later.

One way to develop this habit is to practice focusing on other people and new points of view. Read autobiographies and stories. Take the time to understand why other people act how they do. This includes understanding their value systems, which are not inherently any better or worse than your own.

During day-to-day interactions with others, INTJs will benefit from taking time to question their own judgments. Are you making an effort to understand the other person, their values and their circumstances? Or are you jumping to conclusions and judging before running the situation through your intuition?

When new information appears that could threaten your viewpoint, do you allow it to process or do you get defensive and dismiss it in order to protect your way of seeing the world?

Being very intelligent, INTJs will usually be "right" when it comes to factual situations. Yet, if they do not develop this ability to consider and understand other people, they will suffer in their interpersonal relationships.

As well, they may fail to reach their true potential – all of which would be possible if they were open to new ideas and input from other equally gifted individuals (INTPs, other INTJs, ENTPs, etc.).

## GOING DEEPER EXERCISE

Of the weaknesses listed above, which three do you most recognize in yourself?

_____

_____

_____

_____

_____

What are three weaknesses listed above that you know are having a significant negative impact on your success?

_____

_____

_____

_____

_____

How could you reduce the impact these weaknesses have on your life, either by learning to overcome them or eliminating the activities that bring them to the surface?

_____

_____

_____

_____

_____

# IDEAL CAREER OPTIONS FOR AN INTJ

If you gave a Myers-Briggs test to a group of a few hundred people from the same profession, you would see a very clear pattern.

An accountant in my martial arts class told me that of 600 chartered accountants who took the Myers-Briggs test at his firm, he was one of only three people who didn't score the same type.

This happens for two reasons:

1) Selection Bias: People with the personality type for accounting will tend to do well in related tasks and receive hints that that kind of work is right for them. They may especially enjoy numbers, spreadsheets, etc.
2) Survival Bias: Those with the personality type for accounting are most likely to pass the vigorous tests and internships required to become a chartered accountant.

We are actually much better at finding the right path for us than we give ourselves credit for. In almost every profession, there is a significantly higher percentage of those "typed" to excel in it than random chance would have.

Yet, many people still slip through the cracks, or spend decades searching for that perfect career before finding it.

This chapter will help you avoid the cracks and stop wasting your precious time. Below, you'll find a comprehensive list of careers INTJs tend to be drawn to and succeed in.

There are many more career options beyond this list that I have seen in other books and that intentionally are not included here. These include "good" options that an INTJ could easily do and succeed in, but would not be as happy or fulfilled as they would in another profession where they could use their real strengths.

I have included only the options I believe INTJs have an upper hand in *and* the highest likelihood to find fulfillment and success. There are always other options, but why swim upstream if you don't need to, right?

### To be most successful, an INTJ should focus on work that:

- Allows for creative contribution and problem solving, particularly around existing systems.
- Acknowledges and rewards original thought and ideas with credit going to the INTJ for their contributions.
- Provides enough freedom and autonomy to make changes, develop people, and create systems.
- Happens within a fair and standardized work environment. There should be an established set of criteria used to judge performance so that everyone is compensated fairly (and predictably) based on their contributions.
- Incorporates a high degree of learning. INTJs are always striving to improve their aptitude and add to their skillset. One way they do this is through processing new information and experiences.
- Is set up for independent work but provides the opportunity to collaborate with small groups to bounce ideas off or engage in intellectual discussions.
- Doesn't involve repetitive tasks.
- Allows them to produce work based on their own (usually very high) standards instead of the opinions of others.
- Happens within a friendly and supportive environment with a minimal amount of conflict.

# POPULAR PROFESSIONS FOR INTJs

## Education + Healthcare

- Teacher in sciences, maths, or technology
- Professor
- Administrator
- Mathematician
- Anthropologist
- Curator
- Archivist
- Psychiatrist
- Psychologist
- Neurologist
- Biomedical engineer
- Cardiologist
- Pharmacologist
- Pharmaceutical researcher
- Biomedical researcher
- Coroner
- Pathologist
- Microbiologist
- Geneticist
- Surgeon
- Cardiovascular technician

## In the Business + Professional World

- Telecommunications security
- Management consultant
- Pharmaceutical researcher
- Financial planner
- Investment banker
- International banker
- Strategic planner
- Private sector executive
- Real estate appraiser
- Litigation attorney
- Management consultant
- Intellectual property attorney
- Civil engineer
- Nuclear engineer
- Pilot
- Criminalist and ballistics expert
- Strategic planner
- Investment analyst
- Manager
- Judge

- News analyst
- Engineer

- Metallurgical engineer

## Technology and Computers

- Scientist
- Computer systems analyst
- Technician
- Design engineer
- Astronomer
- Computer programmer
- Environmental planner
- Biomedical researcher
- Biomedical engineer
- Operations research analyst
- Information services developer

- Software and systems developer
- IT services (new business development)
- Network integration specialist
- Computer animator
- Computer engineer
- Java programmer/analyst
- Web developer
- Business analyst
- Software developer
- Computer security specialist

## Creative

- Writer/editorial writer
- Artist
- Inventor
- Graphic designer
- Architect
- Universal design

architect
- Freelance media planner
- Editor/art director
- Columnist, critic, and commentator

## GOING DEEPER EXERCISE

After reading through the list of careers, answer the following questions:

Which 5-10 careers jump out at you as something you'd enjoy doing?

_____

_____

_____

_____

_____

Thinking back to the sections on strengths, what do you notice about the list of careers? What strengths might contribute to success in these careers?

_____

_____

_____

_____

_____

Is your current career, or career path, on the list? If it isn't, how does it stack up against the list of workplace criteria? Could it still be an environment where you find success?

_____

_____

_____

_____

_____

# THRIVING AT WORK

There is an astronomical difference between a job you're good at and a career you love and in which you thrive.

While some people are fine just getting by, people like you and I sure aren't. This section will help you thrive at work.

## THREE FOUNDATIONS FOR THRIVING AT WORK

1) Be aware of your strengths and weaknesses and be selective of the work you do. Be honest in job interviews about where you excel as well as where you struggle.

2) When in a job, take this same honest approach with your supervisor. Explain that you aren't being lazy; rather you feel you could deliver much more *value* to the company by focusing on your strengths.

3) At least once per week, if not daily, stop for a few minutes and ask yourself if you're working in your strengths or struggling in your weaknesses. Remember, you have unique and valuable gifts...but make the effort to use them and avoid getting trapped in the wrong kind of work.

## SECRET WEAPONS AT WORK

When it comes to your work, be sure to tap into these work related strengths for INTJs:

- The ability to see the big picture and understand the consequences of specific approaches or actions.
- The ability to commit and make 'final' decisions (decisiveness) using solid organizational skills.
- Can focus intensely and go deep into one topic, issue, or idea without being distracted.

- Enjoys complex challenges. of an intellectual nature (theories, ideas, etc.).
- Can be objective and think through an issue without taking it personally or letting their own values bias their decision.
- INTJs are intelligent and have no problem focusing. This gives them an ability to grasp difficult ideas and work on one thing until completion.
- The ability to handle rejection well and the ability to maintain their optimism in the face of a challenging situation or setback.
- Independent. Able to jump into a project, take risks, and just do it without much supervision or guidance. This includes having confidence in their ideas and the courage to move forward with them.
- Interested in systems and determining the best way to get things done. Couple this with their strong drive to succeed, and you can understand why INTJs are very good at achieving their goals.
- Is a natural problem solver, always able to come up with a creative solution.
- Internal drive to achieve goals and excel at whatever they do.
- Generally great with technology.

## KRYPTONITE AT WORK

To maximize their success, INTJs should be aware of some challenges they face at work. INTJs will not always, but *may:*

- Easily become bored or sidetracked when the exciting part of a project ends or when confronted by repetitive tasks.
- Impatient with people or organizations they see as uncooperative or ineffective. This can play out as the

employee feeling smarter than the boss and angry that their intelligence and contributions aren't being properly rewarded.

- They may have trouble working with people they see as incompetent.

- Not interested in the mundane details of a project (although they have no problem "following through" in general).

- Be impatient with those who are less creative than them, or those who tend to "ponder" things before making a decision.

- Be stubborn. Once they flex their "decisive" muscle and make a decision, they are reluctant to step backwards and revisit the issue.

- Their ability to focus and commit can manifest itself negatively as inflexibility.

- Can become so theoretical in their thinking that they forget reality; the ideas that come from this thinking then have little or no practical value.

- Can be too tough on others. This includes placing their own high standards on others and neglecting to give praise and appreciation to those they work with. Since the INTJ will often be the smartest person in the room, their words hold considerable weight with their colleagues.

- They often skip the pleasantries as well as the small talk. This can lead others to think they are rude or just don't care (which is not always the case).

- They may give work too much priority in relation to their home life, and neglect other important aspects of their lives.

## GOING DEEPER EXERCISE

Have any of the strengths or weaknesses listed in this chapter been brought to your attention by a boss or colleague before?

_____

_____

_____

_____

_____

Which of the strengths did you instantly recognize in yourself? Are they any you've been underutilizing in your current career?

_____

_____

_____

_____

_____

Which one or two weaknesses, if you were to totally overcome them, would have the greatest positive impact on your career?

_____

_____

_____

_____

_____

# RICH AND HAPPY RELATIONSHIPS

Whoever said opposites attract never met an ENFP + ISTJ couple.

Sure, you want a partner who complements your strengths and weaknesses, but most of us also want someone who understands us; someone to whom we can express our opinions and ideas and be understood.

In this section, we'll start with a discussion on what INTJs are like in relationships. Then we'll look at the most common personality types INTJs are happy with. Lastly, we will provide some advice on creating and maintaining successful relationships as an INTJ and *with* an INTJ.

## INTJs Ideal Matches

A note on compatibility: There is no be all and end all. The information on type compatibility is based either on theory or surveys, neither of which will ever provide a universal rule.

NT (rational) types find the greatest relationship *satisfaction* dating NFs. This is likely because they can share a common way of thinking about the world. With that said, a few of the most compatible matches for INTJs are ENFPs and ENTPs. INTJs will also feel a strong "instant connection" with INFJs.

Ultimately, the two individuals involved, and their desire to grow and work to create an incredible relationship, will have the biggest determination of their success together. The one incompatibility that I've noticed time and time again is between Intuitives (N's) and Sensors (S's). I think this is because these two groups have fundamentally different ways of interacting with the world and often have trouble understanding one another.

In my own experience in romantic relationships, friendships, and business partnerships, I (a strong Intuitive - ENFP), have always run into trouble with those who rate highly on the sensor mode of being.

Beyond that, it's all up in the air. Generally, for organization sake, I would suggest that P's match with a J. The P will benefit from the J's structure and organization, and the J will benefit from the P's creativity and spontaneity.

## TIPS FOR DATING AS AN INTJ

1.  INTJs don't enjoy life's details. Cleaning, organization, scheduling...it's not nearly as appealing as the next big idea. Consider a partner with strengths in these areas to complement you.
2.  INTJs are one of the most independent types and so you're likely low maintenance and value focused time with your ideas and projects. To avoid conflict, you need a confident partner who will give you both emotional freedom and time freedom to do your own thing.
3.  INTJs are excellent partners and loyal companions. Value yourself and what you bring to the table. Take time to access those you date and determine if they can match your standards and meet your expectations.
4.  INTJs don't always know the right thing to say, especially in more intimate or vulnerable moments. It's also common for INTJs to see conflict as more of a logical problem to solve versus the emotional puzzle it really is. Try and make an effort to ask questions and understand the emotions your partner is feeling, otherwise you will be unable to understand the real problem.
5.  If you're after a "perfect" relationship, take time to check in with your partner on this. Do they share your same high

expectations, and if so, is their vision of a "perfect" relationship the same as yours? Communication around these ideas is key to avoiding disappointment.

6. You may set very high expectations for yourself and your partner. Just remember that everyone is human, and no partner or relationship will be perfect. So don't be too hard on your partner, or yourself.

## TIPS FOR DATING AN INTJ

1. INTJs have trouble expressing their feelings. Try and help them along by providing opportunities to casually discuss feelings or situations without judgment. Show them you care and that you're genuinely interested in their happiness.

2. INTJs are not exceptionally well organized, keen on schedules, or great with finances. If you want to build a life with an INTJ, you must accept this and accept them. Develop systems, hire help, or take responsibility for the details of your life together.

3. INTJs spend a lot of their time in their inner world. This world is ripe with creativity and imagination, not to mention the occasional genius. Unfortunately, this means the INTJ isn't always interested in their outer world and may not be present in thought or emotion with those around them. You must know yourself and know if this is the kind of person you will be happy with.

4. INTJs tend to see conflict as a problem they can solve with logic. This might play out much like the typical comedic scene between a man and a woman, with the man trying to solve emotional problems in the same fashion he would repair a car. Be aware that this is simply how your partner's mind is wired and isn't a

reflection of their level of caring. They care about you; they just try and solve problems rationally. Make an effort to explain how you feel and how what they say impacts you, as they might not actually know.

5. INTJs are very confident and independent. This can be a good or a bad thing, depending on your own needs. Just know that they need their space and will have no problem keeping themselves entertained whenever you're apart.

To learn more about how all the types relate and interact, download the free compatibility chart at:

www.PersonalityTypesTraining.com/thrive

# MORE ADVICE FROM INTJS FOR INTJS

*"I'm 29, but I've been working actively on myself since I was 14 and was told by family, teachers, and friends that my social skills were below par as I was "too logical." At 16, my grades dropped significantly because I rebelled against teachers as I felt the rules were not logical enough. It got me nowhere. Sometimes rules are just rules for the sake of it; just follow them as they are not permanent. Low grades ruin everything before you even get to the fun stuff.*

*"At 18, I ruined a good long-time relationship with being too logical and not taking into account the reality of the other (his feelings). Logic does not mend heartbreak.*

*"At 20, I learned how to quit my university studies as, even though it made sense, my heart wasn't in it. I changed my study topic, but lost two years of study time (and money). I felt it was too illogical to follow my heart.*

*"At 22, I didn't know when to quit a very bad relationship, as it sounded good on paper. My heart got squished anyway, and I felt like an idiot for not quitting when I had the chance. Looking back, logic made the after-shock even worse ('but I should have seen the signs ... it was too obvious. Wow, I feel stupid!'). There is such a thing as counterproductive logic.*

*"At 25, I finally found my passion while writing my Master's dissertation: I loved statistics, writing, and researching; I thought everyone liked it; it was logical to me. It's not. It's okay to have a passion for nerdy things, or really odd things, or something really, really stupid (like loving to dance when you're alone and not with people around).*

*"At 27, I started my PhD on an interesting topic, which left enough room to be creative with my skills.*

*"At 29, I couldn't be happier.*

*"First, social skills are more important than you might think: Learning the social rules of different surroundings is more difficult for us than it is for others, as it involves taking into account the feelings of others. Feelings are not logical: You need to accept other people's feelings even though they do not make sense. If they feel a certain way, then that is their reality, whether or not you agree with them. There is not one reality; we all have our own version.*

*"Secondly, don't expect others to play by the rules like we do (whether it is in business, the dating world, etc.). About half the living beings do not play fair and do not stick to the rules (or the law, or...). I'm not saying not to follow the rules (because we're not practiced in it, we end up drawing attention to us, making rule breaking even harder), but to take into account that others might not play fair.*

*"Thirdly, refrain from dropping scientific facts in discussions you are not partaking in. Only do this if you are ASKED to join in on the discussion. Discussions are sometimes not at all about the topic,*

*but about the people involved! This might seem strange to you. If you are not able to feel when this is the case (I know I can't), stay out of the discussion. These kinds of 'personal' discussions can become very irrational, and if you partake, you might end up being viewed as 'being on their side,' or against them. Social situations are a lot more complicated than we would think.*

*"Fourth, watch the attitude. You are NOT the best at something; there is always someone better than you. If you feel like you are the best person to answer a question, always weigh your words. Put in a 'most of the time,' or a 'very likely.' There can always be someone who's an expert waiting to answer. There will always be different opinions. Yes, even in science. Especially in science, actually.*

*"Fifth, look for a job you truly enjoy, even if you have to change a lot of careers. As an INTJ, your work is extremely important, so make sure you are enjoying it. And 'enjoying it' does not mean all day, every day. Every job has administration or mind-numbing parts.*

*"Sixth, know when to quit. Whether it's a discussion with someone who turns irrational, or a game where someone doesn't play fair, or a relationship that seems rational but isn't what you hoped for. If it's not fun anymore, and it's taking a toll by continuing, quit. This might be problematic advice for youngsters who usually quit before giving it a go, but an INTJ needs to be pushed to quit. We continue doing something because it sounds logical,*

*because it seems like the right thing to do, etc. Sometimes you just have to quit."*

*"Know yourself, love yourself, respect yourself, take the time to truly understand what it means to do so and actually do it."*

*"Although, I'm neither old nor wise, I can offer you some advice from C. Hitchens, who is someone I admire greatly. The advice has quite an INTJ character.*

*"Beware the irrational, however seductive. Shun the transcendent and all who invite you to subordinate or annihilate yourself. Distrust compassion; prefer dignity for yourself and others. Don't be afraid to be thought arrogant or selfish. Picture all experts as if they were mammals. Never be a spectator of unfairness or stupidity. Seek out argument and disputation for their own sake; the grave will supply plenty of time for silence. Suspect your own motives, and all excuses. Do not live for others any more than you would expect others to live for you.'"*

*"Follow your intuition more than outsiders' advice to take more chances on fulfilling your dreams. Others, and even well-meaning others, will always hold you back." (My 2 cents)*

*"Be clear but not rude with your boundaries. Beware of skilled passive-aggressives and people who excel at lying to themselves, they screw up your 'human radar.'"*

*"I would say: Friends are important. You don't need many, but try to get at least one very close friend (for emotional chat, or for exchanging personal ideas), and get some semi-regular friends in case you want to go to a movie, etc. Actually, invest time and effort into these relationships, as there WILL be a time you would prefer company; even introverted people need a good social time once in a while.*

*"If you have a very difficult time socializing and making new friends, look for a common interest group. Sure, it's what it says everywhere, but really LOOK: online, in a local newspaper, etc.*

*"For example, if you like playing board games, look for a group that comes together for board games. There are groups for everything, however daft the interest might sound. Just LOOK.*

*"I myself go to a games group. It took me a month to work up the courage to just show up there alone, as I knew no one. I waited outside in my car like a complete idiot, terrified of going in. Every logical thought in me came up screaming, telling me what a terrible idea it was, trying to convince myself. I texted a friend, who told me I was being a complete idiot (really, get one of those kinds of friends who*

*are utterly honest to you, you can't do without one!), and I got out of the car.*

*"Once I got inside, trembling to my core, standing there in the middle of the room for what must have been only a few seconds but felt like ages, someone came up to me, asked if I was there for games, and it took me five minutes to get settled in after being introduced. I realized the room was just FILLED (well, there's only 10 of us, but it seems full) with introverted people like me, who just like playing games and don't have others in their family who like it on a regular basis. Their spouses/friends are usually the ones dragging them along, so there will always be a few extroverted feeling people there, who understand it's difficult for someone like us to show up. I've been going for two years now, and I've actually made new friends quite easily. Sure, I wouldn't call them if I were in trouble, but they are 'game friends.'*

*"It's also a great way to meet new people for dating. Even if there's no one there you like at that moment, they might bring their friends to those groups. That's the cool thing about creepy-new social circles: You never know.... Plus, if you don't meet someone, you're still having fun.*

*"Social situations in general: Push yourself once in a while. Talk to someone waiting for a bus or train, go to a local thing you might enjoy (an art show, a fair, a concert, etc.), maybe finally learn to paint ... or study that one language that always interested you (Russian is a fun one ... difficult, but fun!).*

*"Up until now, the best opportunities (work, school, love, friends, etc.) for me have come from those occasional pushes. I'm not saying you have to become extroverted and deny who you are. Just push yourself once in a while, so you don't close yourself off like a hermit. You are very likely to meet other hermits-to-be. Maybe not immediately the first time, but you will!"*

# KEYS TO WEALTH, HEALTH, HAPPINESS, AND SUCCESS

I hope this book has provided some insights into how you can succeed in the most important areas of your life.

In this last section, I'd like to share ten important strategies for you to remember that will help you create a balanced and happy life. If you apply them, these strategies will help you enjoy more wealth, health, and happiness in your life.

1.  INTJs must follow their strengths and do work that is aligned with their abilities. Take on work that will reward you for your ability to think big, create strategic plans, and follow through to success.

2.  Be accountable and take personal responsibility. It is important to be aware of your weaknesses, but do not use this knowledge as an excuse. Never blame others. When you blame others for your circumstances, you give away the power to change them. Take responsibility for your life and you give yourself the power to change it.

3.  INTJs really dislike repetitive work, so stick to "project based" work that allows you to focus on one idea - from the light bulb moment through to execution and completion.

4.  Plan and schedule time to be around people. When alone for too long, INTJs can get lost in their own thoughts and lose connection with the outside world.

5.  Learn to understand others. You have a unique and wonderful way of looking at the world...but it is one of

many ways, and no more right than any others. Learn to understand how other people see the world and your influence will increase while the amount of conflict in your world decreases.

6. INTJs are often far too hard on themselves and those close to them. You have very high standards for yourself and that's good. But comparing yourself or others to a lofty vision can lead to harsh and unfair judgments that won't contribute to your success. Take time to review accomplishments, progress, and positive traits.

   If you're feeling down on yourself, don't be afraid to express these thoughts to others around you and allow them to flatter you with kind words.

7. Make an effort to praise and show appreciation for those around you. You may be very confident and self-assured, but not everyone is. A few kind words from you can go a long way towards motivating those you work with and lifting the spirits of the people you care about.

8. Focus on goals that will bring a balanced happiness to your life.

9. Make time to spend with people and allow your mind to relax. Often it is during this "down time" that the best ideas are formulated.

10. It's easy to get trapped in your head or your ideas. Start a hobby or activity that involves something physical, such as a sport, outdoor activity, or artistic craft. This will help you get out of your head and connect your ideas with the world around you.

## PRACTICAL SOLUTIONS TO COMMON CHALLENGES

There is an old-fashioned attitude that tells us to just tough it up, overcome our weaknesses, and do everything ourselves.

This is stupid.

If you're an exceptional painter you should spend your time painting and leave the toilet cleaning to someone else. If you struggle with negotiation, there is nothing wrong with asking a friend or partner to come along and offer support.

The more you allow yourself to offload the tasks and responsibilities you don't enjoy, the more success you will experience. Here are a few practical ideas for making the most of your strengths while avoiding your weaknesses.

As an INTJ, you'll benefit from hiring help with day-to-day chores such as cleaning, laundry, yard work, and maintenance. It's not that you can't do these things, it's just that your time is much more valuable elsewhere.

The only exception would be if you actually enjoy any of these tasks, such as mowing the lawn, and find it therapeutic or an opportunity to think over ideas.

# IMPROVING YOUR SOCIAL SKILLS

## SOCIAL SKILLS TRAINING AND ADVICE ON SOCIAL SITUATIONS

*When I published the first version of this book, I had many readers contact me and ask for more advice around social situations. The following sections are simply a response to this request and not an assertion that INTJs need this advice or haven't already figured it out.*

*So, if you already consider yourself a social butterfly, you may feel free to skip this section.*

### Social Skills Training and Advice on Social Situations

In our always-on, always-connected society of email, text messaging, and, well, anything but face-to-face conversation, social situations can be a challenge for anyone. We merely do not have as many opportunities to practice conversation as we used to.

As an introvert, INTJs enjoy time alone and are around others even less than their extrovert counterparts. This means even less time for the natural practice and development of social skills.

Does this mean introverts are doomed to a life of awkward interactions and social anxiety? Absolutely not. In fact, it is quite the contrary.

When they invest time into developing their social skills, introverts can become just as capable in social situations as extroverts. This gives them a well-rounded personality and an excellent advantage: the ability to chat and socialize when they want, and to sit quietly and listen to others when the situation calls for it. No one likes the person who always has to be the center of attention, right?

This chapter is broken into seven sections, each covering a particular social skill or social situation. At the end of the chapter, you will find a list of additional resources to help you continue working on your social skills.

## BEING INTERESTED

I have heard it said that being interested in others is the fastest route to becoming the most interesting person in the room. Show a genuine interest in others and you will be well liked.

When you take an interest in another person, a few powerful things happen.

1 - You build rapport and the other person starts to like you.

2 - You learn important details about the other person. You can then use these details to create conversation around common interests.

When learning about another person, what you ask is almost as important as how you ask it. Typical small talk questions like "So what do you do?" are as boring as they are uninformative. Try using some of the questions below and you will find yourself in much more stimulating conversations.

- What is your biggest goal for this year?
- (Can be followed up by: Why? What challenges do you see coming up?)
- What is your favorite part about your career/hobby/relationship/hometown?
- What is the biggest challenge you are currently facing in your work/school/life?
- I have noticed that you are really good at (insert

something you have noticed – for example their style, conversation, telling jokes, business, or cooking). What is your secret? Could you share two or three tips for an amateur like me?

When you are asking questions about their goals or challenges, you are giving yourself an opportunity to offer advice or help them find a solution. You will be amazed at how far this can go, and how much more stimulating the conversation can become when you are working on solving a problem.

In terms of how you approach this, just be curious and thoughtful in your mindset and you will do just fine.

## GETTING OUTSIDE OF YOURSELF

The curious thing is that most people at social events are all thinking the same thing: "I wonder what other people are thinking about me."

When you come to realize and truly accept this, everything changes. If you are friendly and kind, you will be amazed at how many people will be drawn to you (especially other introverts!).

Of course, much of our anxiety in social situations goes back to the same question playing in our heads: "I wonder what others are thinking about me."

How do you get past this? Look no further than the last tip: Be genuinely interested in other people. When you move your focus to understanding and caring about others, it is almost impossible to focus on yourself at the same time.

## SAY SOMETHING PLEASANT

One compliment can, and will, change someone's whole night.

So why don't we give people more compliments? One reason is that we get stuck in our heads, wondering what to say and how to say it. We worry about coming off as inauthentic, offending someone, or appearing like a kiss ass. We wonder whether our compliment could be misinterpreted, or get us into an awkward situation. Although all these fears are normal, they are also all unfounded.

The key to giving an excellent compliment is in the details, so pay attention to them. Some people spend hours picking out their outfits - nothing is left to chance. Sometimes there will be an obvious "point of pride," such as a new dress or piece of jewelry the person is just waiting to be complimented on. Other times it might not be so obvious, so try these tips:

- For a man, his watch or tie is always a safe compliment (from a man or a woman). From a woman to a man, well, you can get away with complimenting anything.
- For women, jewelry, purses, and shoes are always a point of pride and a safe compliment from another woman.

For the guys, it is a little more complicated. If you don't know the woman well, keep it casual in what you compliment and how you say it. Fashionable jewelry, a trendy phone case, or a colorful watch are safe bets and good conversation starters. Follow up your compliment by asking where they got it, or if there is a groovy story behind it. For example: "That's a really cool watch. Is there a story behind it?"

If you already know the woman, a new hairstyle or piece of clothing is also begging for your compliment.

- Always be as authentic as possible. Look for something you do like in someone, whether it is something physical or a character trait. You will never upset someone by mentioning their excellent sense of humor.
- Sometimes you will be able to notice an area someone is trying to improve and is perhaps self-conscious about. For instance, you may notice a fellow introvert making a big effort to be social and telling a story to a group of people. This is an amazing opportunity...use it.

It's not hard to say, "That was really funny, you know. You are a wonderful storyteller." Yet a few kind words on your part here could make an unforgettable impact and go a long way in building their confidence and encouraging them to continue growing. In doing so, not only do you make someone else feel great, you also make them feel good about you.

## PLEASE AND THANK YOU

One of the challenges many introvert types face is a dislike of doing things "just because," particularly when it comes to social norms and etiquette. To the outside world, it can appear as rude or inconsiderate when an INTJ does not say thank you to their host for having them over for dinner. In reality, the INTJ may be very appreciative, they just don't see the need for pleasantries (or they just forgot). They may also take it for granted, assuming the other person knows how much they care about them, or assuming a close friend does not need to be thanked.

The problem is that some people are overly sensitive or just stuck in their ways. Sometimes a lack of "etiquette" can cause unnecessary hostility or conflict, especially with those who do not know you as well, such as a good friend's spouse.

Two things you can do:

**Option 1:** Make an effort to build habits around manners and etiquette. Perhaps it does not make sense to thank someone for passing the salt, but just do it anyway.

**Option 2:** Take a few minutes to speak to, or write a note to, the most important people in your life. Tell them how much you value your relationship and explain to them that social norms are not exactly your thing. Make it clear how much you value them and everything they do for you, even if you do not express it at the moment they do it.

Once a year, say around Christmas, send out handwritten cards to your closest friends and make sure to include a note about how much you appreciate them and how happy you are that they are part of your life.

If you do these two things, not only will they not care when you forget a "thank you," you will stand out as one of the most caring and thoughtful people they know.

## EXPLAINING NERVES AND SOCIAL ANXIETY

As we walked into one of our regular cafés, my girlfriend reminded me to say hi to her friend working there. "She was upset that you did not say goodbye last time."

This sparked a conversation on "hi and bye" etiquette, and approaching people working or in a group. I explained that most of the time when someone does not come over and say hi they are not trying to be rude. Usually there is something else going on. Often this something else is nervousness or social anxiety. Approaching a group of people to say hello when you only know one or two of them can cause much stress. Logically, it probably should not, but alas, it does. One option is to face the nerves and awkwardly approach the group, while you stand there waiting to be invited to sit or for the right time to walk away. The other option is a brief wave, or to pretend you did not see them, and move on. In this case you risk being considered rude, or having people think you do not like them, or are mad at them.

Isn't it funny, the wide gap between two people's perceptions?

Unfortunately, there is no magic cure for this situation, although, for the sake of personal growth, I would encourage you to try to say hello whenever possible.

Although there is no magic cure, there is a way you can limit the potential damage (and possibly make the situation a lot easier in the future).

The solution is along the same lines as the one in the "Please and Thank You" section. You need to initiate an honest discussion with friends. For an extreme introvert, the idea of being nervous about approaching a group of people is almost confusing. To them, the only possible explanation is rudeness or a disinterest in them.

Yet guess what happens when you explain the situation from your point of view? They start to understand. Not only will they "get it" when you do not approach them within a group, they may even spot you and come to say hello first.

**Note:** In this section, I use the term social anxiety to describe nervousness or anxiety around situations. If the negative emotions are so strong that they negatively influence your life, or the anxiety is constant, we may be talking about a more serious form of social anxiety. If this sounds like you, I encourage you to read: Self-Confidence Secrets: How To Overcome Anxiety, Fear, and Low Self-Esteem With NLP.

I have received many emails from readers telling me that this book has helped them overcome (sometimes crippling) social anxiety and build their confidence.

Find it on Amazon.com

## AVOID CRITICIZING AND COMPLAINING

You are at a social event and you feel uncomfortable. You didn't really want to go in the first place, and now you are dreading your decision to "give it a try." You find yourself at the bar when a fellow guest, equally disappointed, strikes up a conversation with you:

"Why are these things always so boring? This might be the worst one yet."

Now it is your turn to speak. How do you respond?

It is easy to fall into this negativity trap. Being critical of others is one of the easiest ways to feel better about yourself (in the moment) and temporarily bond with others. The problem is that it's a short-term solution with many negative long-term consequences. Complaining and criticizing brings you down emotionally, eliminates any drive to become more social, and almost guarantees the night will not get any better.

What is more? When you become a complainer, you repel the people you would have the most fun talking with and the ones who are likely in charge of deciding who will get invited back.

Sure, in that moment, never being invited back may sound like a blessing. Would it not be better to get invited back and just decline the invitation if you do not want to go?

## ESCAPING THE SMALL TALK TRAP: DIRECT THE CONVERSATION, ASK QUESTIONS, AND GET HELP

Nothing is worse than the *Small Talk Trap*. You are at a social event where you hardly know anyone and find yourself in a conversation with a stranger. Initially, the conversation provides relief from the awkward agony of "working the room," but soon the conversation is just as painful. You find yourself thinking back to biology class, wondering how much long-term damage would come from jumping out the second story window behind you and making a run for it.

*It doesn't have to be like this! There is a better way.*

Here are three skills you can use to make your conversations more stimulating.

**Strategy #1 - Direct It.** There is a good chance the other person does not want to talk about the weather any more than you do. Even if they do, why leave it up to them?

When you go to an event, have a few thought-provoking conversation topics in mind. Ideally, these should be interesting to you and the kind of people you like to talk to. An example could be a book you just read about another culture or a philosophy you have been studying. When the weather comes up for the third time in a conversation, it is time to change it with this simple phrase:

"Hey, sorry to interrupt, but I would love your opinion on something before I forget. I have been reading this book on Stoic philosophy and it has been bombarding me with ideas about how to live life. I keep wondering how these ideas can relate to our modern lifestyle. Do you know much about Stoicism?"

At this point, they might be familiar with the topic. That's excellent. If they are not, it is a chance for you to explain it to them. In doing so, you will crystalize your knowledge of the topic and hopefully teach them something interesting in the process.

Sure, some will not have a lot to say, but others will. Either way, you will have a much better time in this conversation than one about weather or sports!

**Strategy #2 - Ask Questions.** Most people have at least one worthwhile trait or area of knowledge. If you find yourself trapped in a painful conversation, use it as your chance to learn something new.

Start by asking a few quick background questions about the person's home country, work, and hobbies. From there you will be able to find something thought-provoking to zero in on and learn more about. Are they from a far-off country you have always wanted to know more about? Turn this into an opportunity to learn a few phrases in a new language, to discover a few cultural differences, or ask about possible economic opportunities. Perhaps they study a martial art you have always wanted to learn. You could ask them for advice on the best way to get started, and how to spend your time in this activity for the first three months.

It won't always be the most fascinating conversation you've ever had, but it's still better than typical small talk.

**Strategy #3 - Get Help.** This one can be trickier, but once mastered, is a ninja skill of social situations. If you are speaking one-on-one with someone and the conversation is leaving a lot to be desired, try to bring in another person.

The easiest way to do this is when you spot someone you know, or a stranger standing alone, and just motion for them to join you. If this is not an option, there is always Plan B. Take the conversation to a point where you need an opinion on something. Perhaps you decide to disagree on what city has the best weather, or which appetizer at the party is best. Whatever it is, use it as an opportunity to seek another opinion from someone walking or standing nearby: "Excuse me, we were just debating this and would love another opinion. What do you think ...?"

However you do it, two things can happen when you bring in a new person:

One, they could be a stimulating conversationalist and change your night for the better. Often, when this happens, your original conversation partner will eventually excuse themselves and you will be left with an enjoyable conversation and possibly a new friend. If the conversation does not improve, at least you have given yourself a less awkward escape route because you will not be leaving anyone alone.

Another upside of this approach is that you may be saving someone else from the awkwardness of standing alone, and they will be grateful for it.

## ADDITIONAL RESOURCES ON SOCIAL SKILLS

If you enjoyed this section and want to continue your study of people and social skills, here are a few books to get you started.

- Networking for People Who Hate Networking: A Field Guide for Introverts, the Overwhelmed, and the Underconnected
- Self-Promotion for Introverts: The Quiet Guide to Getting Ahead
- The Introverted Leader: Building on Your Quiet Strength
- Quiet: The Power of Introverts in a World That Can't Stop Talking
- Quiet Influence: The Introvert's Guide to Making a Difference
- The Introvert Advantage: Making the Most of Your Inner Strengths

# INSIGHTS INTO THE INTJ PERSONALITY

This chapter is a contribution from a very insightful and well thought-out reader who goes by the name of Rick Wolf. Rick is also an INTJ.

Enter Rick here.

---

For a jumpstart on how to deal with an INTJ, visit:

http://intjcentral.com/the-compleat-idiots-guide-to-the-intj/

Everything there is true, all of it. Now I'll share my thoughts.

INTJs, being blunt, introverted perfectionists, start out as one of the most socially awkward MBTI types. Growing up, many feel angst and turmoil as they feel the social expectation from family and peers to be popular, have friends, and have an active social life. Hormones will further charge their drive to meet the opposite sex well before they have mastered their social skills.

I took an employment test and was so curious about the results that I tracked down a professional who interpreted the results for me. He said he knew that I would find him. He didn't tell me much more beyond that, but his comment drove me to find out more about personality tests, which in turn led me to the MBTI.

**Immature INTJs see feelings as a weakness.** It won't be until they are near full development of their personalities, if ever, that they will realize how very wrong they are. Until then, they can be a terror to deal with. Once they understand the value of emotions, feelings, and principles, they tend to make great contributions to society and find fulfillment. They also start to see the value and recognize the contributions of feeler types.

**INTJs may be just as big of slobs as their INTP cousins.**
Where they differ is that they will have a well thought-out system to get them through life without constantly forgetting their lunch, gym bag, tasks, appointments, and pants. I am as forgetful as they come, but I will have my morning get-out-the-door system tattooed on my forearm before I am ever late for work. The weird thing is, as important as it is that I be at work on time, I will be out the door three minutes early so that I beat traffic and can set my cruise control and not be stuck behind some schmuck foolishly going the speed limit. **Efficiency is the INTJ mantra.**

INTJs always have a schedule. Even on weekends. It can be completely arbitrary, but once it is set in the INTJ's mind it might as well be set in stone. If you want to have a conversation with said INTJ, it is best to schedule it, preferably by email.

INTJs will be much more thankful for the beginning of the school semester than most types. OK, they might be the only ones. To an INTJ, learning equals dopamine (the reward chemical caused by orgasms).

Funerals are the bane of the INTJ and not because there is a dead person in the room. The INTJ is very uncomfortable with displays of emotion. INTJs are very confused by tradition. Funerals mix both, and to top it off the INTJ may have their own emotions that they are trying to keep bottled up to prevent anyone from seeing a crack in their Vulcan-like exterior. Add to that Aunt Eunice crying so hard you can see her makeup running as she pulls you in for a hug. It is a wonder there aren't more INTJs faking a heart attack to get out early. In cases like this, it is helpful to bring a non-INTJ, preferably someone that is Fe dominant, to advise you on proper protocol and force you to stay for the appropriate amount of time, by gunpoint if necessary. Weddings are very similar, but much, much worse.

# QUOTES TO MAKE AN INTJ SMILE

To end with, I've included a collection of fun, inspiring, and relatable quotes for INTJs. Many are from INTJs; others are simply enjoyable for INTJs.

To make them easier to read and ponder, I've formatted them to be one quote per page.

*"I also believe that introversion is my greatest strength. I have such a strong inner life that I'm never bored and only occasionally lonely. No matter what mayhem is happening around me, I know I can always turn inward."*

### -SUSAN CAIN

*"I have always imagined that Paradise will be a kind of library."*

### -JORGE LUIS BORGES

*"A common quality I see of people who are successful is that they are voracious readers."*

### -MATT MULLENWEG

*"The individual has always had to struggle to keep from being overwhelmed by the tribe. To be your own man is a hard business. If you try it, you'll be lonely often, and sometimes frightened. But no price is too high to pay for the privilege of owning yourself."*

## -RUDYARD KIPLING

*"I read a book one day and my whole life was changed."*

## -ORHAN PAMUK

*"It's always better to leave the party early."*

## -BILL WATTERSON

*"The third-rate mind is only happy when it is thinking with the majority. The second-rate mind is only happy when it is thinking with the minority. The first-rate mind is only happy when it is thinking."*

## -A.A. MILNE

*"That which can be asserted without evidence, can be dismissed without evidence."*

## -CHRISTOPHER HITCHENS

*"You can't convince a believer of anything; for their belief is not based on evidence, it's based on a deep-seated need to believe."*

**-CARL SAGAN**

*"The mind is sharper and keener in seclusion and uninterrupted solitude. No big laboratory is needed in which to think. Originality thrives in seclusion free of outside influences beating upon us to cripple the creative mind. Be alone, that is the secret of invention; be alone, that is when ideas are born."*

**-NIKOLA TESLA**

*"When people believe a conclusion is true, they are also very likely to believe arguments that appear to support it, even when these arguments are unsound."*

**-DANIEL KAHNEMAN**

*"Our minds are finite and far from noble. Knowing their limits can help us to become better reasoners."*

**-GARY MARCUS**

*"The core of a scientific lifestyle is to change your mind when faced with information that disagrees with your views, avoiding intellectual inertia, yet many of us praise leaders who stubbornly stick to their views as 'strong.'"*

**-MAX TEGMARK**

*"Contrary to what our brains are telling us, there's no mystical force that imbues a winner with a streak of luck, nor is there a cosmic sense of justice that ensures that a loser's luck will turn around. The universe doesn't care one whit whether you've been winning or losing; each roll of the dice is just like every other."*

**-CHARLES SEIFE**

*"The mediocrity principle simply states that you aren't special. The universe does not revolve around you; this planet isn't privileged in any unique way; your country is not the perfect product of directed, intentional fate; and that tuna sandwich you had for lunch was not plotting to give you indigestion."*

**-P.Z. MYERS**

*"There are no walls, no bolts, no locks that anyone can put on your mind."*

### -OTTO FRANK

*"Reality is that which, when you stop believing in it, doesn't go away."*

### -PHILIP K. DICK

*"It is the mark of an educated mind to be able to entertain a thought without accepting it."*

### -ARISTOTLE

*"The trouble with the world is that the stupid are cocksure and the intelligent are full of doubt."*

### -BERTRAND RUSSELL

*"Everyone is entitled to his own opinion, but not his own facts."*

### -DANIEL PATRICK MOYNIHAN

*"Facts do not cease to exist because they are ignored."*

### -ALDOUS HUXLEY

*"Sometimes I get so excited by the infinite possibilities of the future that I forget I'm building them here in the present."*

### -WAYNE LIN

*"If you want to assert a truth, first make sure it's not just an opinion that you desperately want to be true."*

### -NEIL DEGRASSE TYSON

*"People confuse bluntness with bitchiness."*

### -JULIA STILES

*"People call me a perfectionist, but I'm not. I'm a rightist. I do something until it's right."*

### -JAMES CAMERON

*"My goal is simple. It is a complete understanding of the universe."*

### -STEPHEN HAWKING

*"Without a goal [maneuvering is] aimless. You might be a master tactician, but you'll have no sense of strategy."*

### -GARRY KASPAROV

*"Short-term satisfaction will never lead to something timeless."*

### -JACK DORSEY

*"Great things are not done by impulse, but by a series of small things brought together."*

### -GEORGE ELIOT

*"Whenever you find yourself on the side of the majority, it is time to pause and reflect."*

### -MARK TWAIN

*"I have no idols. I admire work, dedication and competence."*

### -AYRTON SENNA

*"Be less curious about people and more curious about ideas."*

### -MARIE CURIE

*"I'd like to show an improved product rather than just talk about things we might do."*

### -MARK ZUCKERBERG

*"People who think they know everything are a great annoyance to those of us who do."*

**-ISAAC ASIMOV**

*"Take the risk of thinking for yourself; much more happiness, truth, beauty, and wisdom will come to you that way."*

**-CHRISTOPHER HITCHENS**

*"If I have done the public any service, it is due to my patient thought."*

**-ISAAC NEWTON**

*"As for the right way, the correct way, and the only way, it does not exist."*

**-FRIEDRICH NIETZSCHE**

*"I never did give anybody hell. I just told the truth and they thought it was hell."*

**-HARRY S. TRUMAN**

*"Impossible is a word to be found only in the dictionary of fools."*

**-NAPOLEON BONAPARTE**

# NEXT STEPS

To help you get the most from this book, I have created a collection of free extras to support you along the way. If you haven't done so already, take a few minutes now to request the free bonuses; you already paid for them when you bought this book. To download these, simply visit the special section of my website: www.PersonalityTypesTraining.com/thrive

There you will be asked to enter your email address so I can send you the "Thriving Bonus Pack." You'll receive:

1.  A 5-part mini-course (delivered via email) with tips on how to adjust your life so you can best make use of your strengths.
2.  A compatibility chart showing how you are most likely to relate to the other 15 personality types. You'll discover which types are most compatible with you and which types will likely lead to headaches.
3.  A PDF workbook that complements this book. It's formatted to be printed, so you can fill in your answers to the exercises in each chapter as you go.

To download the Thriving Bonus Pack, visit:

www.PersonalityTypesTraining.com/thrive

# SUGGESTIONS AND FEEDBACK

Like the field of psychology, this book will always be growing and improving.

If there's something about this book you didn't like, or there is a point you disagreed with, I'd love to hear from you. Perhaps I missed something in my research.

As well, if you're an "experienced" INTJ and you'd like to add your personal story, insight, wisdom, or advice to upcoming editions, my readers and I would love to hear from you.

To contribute in any way, you can email me at: me@thedanjohnston.com.

# A SMALL FAVOR

If you've enjoyed this book or found it useful, I'd be very grateful if you'd post a short review on Amazon. Your support really does make a difference. I read all the reviews personally, so I can get your feedback and make this book even better.

If you'd like to leave a review then all you need to do is visit this book's page on Amazon.

Thanks again for your support!

# OTHER BOOKS ABOUT INFPS AND THEIR MOST COMPATIBLE TYPES: ENTJS AND ENFJS

**INTJ: Lessons from the Unstoppable Mastermind**

Or just visit Amazon and search for "INTJ". Then look for the book by Dan Johnston.

**ENFP: The Inspiring Champion**

Or just visit Amazon and search for "ENFP". Then look for the book by Dan Johnston.

### ENTP: The Charming and Visionary Inventor

Or just visit Amazon and search for "ENTP". Then look for the book by Dan Johnston.

### ENFP: Inspired and Inspiring

Or just visit Amazon and search for "ENFP". Then look for the book by Dan Johnston.

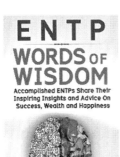

### ENTP: Words of Wisdom

Or just visit Amazon and search for "ENTP". Then look for the book by Dan Johnston..

# BOOKS IN THE THRIVE PERSONALITY TYPE SERIES

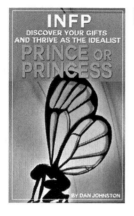

### INFP: The Prince or Princess

Or just visit Amazon and search for "INFP". Then look for the book by Dan Johnston.

### ENFJ: The Leader, Teacher, and People Person

Or just visit Amazon and search for "ENFJ". Then look for the book by Dan Johnston.

### INFJ: The Protector and Most Disciplined Of Idealists

Or just visit Amazon and search for "INFJ". Then look for the book by Dan Johnston.

### ENTJ: The Unstoppable Fieldmarshal and Executive

Or just visit Amazon and search for "ENTJ". Then look for the book by Dan Johnston.

### INTP: The Often Genius Thinker and Architect

Or just visit Amazon and search for "INTP". Then look for the book by Dan Johnston.

## THRIVE SERIES COLLECTIONS

**The Idealists: Learning To Thrive As, and With, ENFPs, INFPs, ENFJs, and INFJs**

A Collection of Four Books from the Thrive Series.

**The Rationals: Learning To Thrive As, and With, The INTJ, ENTJ, INTP, and ENTP Personality Types**

A Collection of Four Books from the Thrive Series.

# ABOUT THE AUTHOR

Dan Johnston is a #1 international best-selling author, speaker, coach, and recognized expert in the fields of confidence, psychology, and personal transformation. As a coach, one of his specialties is helping clients discover their natural talents, apply them to their true purpose, and create a plan of action to live the life of their dreams.

Dan has been a student of psychology, personal change, and social interaction for over a decade. His passion for helping others feel and be their best drives his continuous pursuit to understand exactly how people work.

Dan's educational background includes a degree in Psychology from a world-renowned university, training with Anthony Robbins at his Leadership Academy, and NLP Practitioner Training with Harry Nichols.

In his personal life, Dan has turned his dreams into reality. Between 2012 and 2013 he lived in five new places: Costa Rica, New York, Germany, Italy, and Spain. Today Dan calls Germany his home base but insists that "home" is wherever he hangs his hat for the week. He frequently travels throughout Europe. Dan spends his mornings writing new books and his early evenings on Skype working one-on-one with his coaching clients, supporting them in creating their own dream lives.

**To learn more about Dan Johnston, or inquire about life and business coaching with him, please visit:**

www.DreamsAroundTheWorld.com/coaching

For free articles, interviews, and resources on entrepreneurship, pursuing your passions, travel, and creating the life of your dreams, visit Dreams Around The World and subscribe to the "Business Takeoff Training":

**www.DreamsAroundTheWorld.com**

**Find more books by Dan Johnston on his Amazon Author Central Pages:**

Amazon.com:

http://www.amazon.com/author/danjohnston

Amazon.co.uk:

http://www.amazon.co.uk/-/e/B00E1DO6OS

Made in the USA
Middletown, DE
10 August 2016